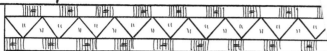

Rardee

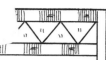

D0890923

Listen and Color
NATIVE AMERICAN LEGENDS
Book and CD

Illustrated by
JOHN GREEN

DOVER PUBLICATIONS, INC.
Mineola, New York

Bibliographical Note

Listen and Color: Native American Legends Book and CD is a new work, first published by Dover Publications, Inc., in 2004.

DOVER *Pictorial Archive* SERIES

This book belongs to the Dover Pictorial Archive Series. You may use the designs and illustrations for graphics and crafts applications, free and without special permission, provided that you include no more than four in the same publication or project. (For permission for additional use, please write to Permissions Department, Dover Publications, Inc., 31 East 2nd Street, Mineola, N.Y. 11501.)

However, republication or reproduction of any illustration by any other graphic service, whether it be in a book or in any other design resource, is strictly prohibited.

International Standard Book Number: 0-486-43892-9

Manufactured in the United States of America
Dover Publications, Inc., 31 East 2nd Street, Mineola, N.Y. 11501

NOTE

The ten Native American legends illustrated in this book represent a sampling of stories handed down through generations of various indigenous peoples of North America: the Tsimshian Indians of the Pacific Northwest; the Passamaquoddy of Maine and the Micmac of New Brunswick; the Pueblo of the American Southwest; the Cherokee, the Iroquois, and the Sioux. Many of these legends explain natural phenomena or feature mischievous beings who can change shape at will. Also included are legends of the strange and wonderful, such as "The Friendly Skeleton," a story that takes us to an enchanted island where the dead come to life.

In this entertaining coloring book and CD set, youngsters can color forty scenes from Native American folklore while listening to ten authentic myths and legends. With the audio compact disc found on the inside back cover, listeners can learn about North America's original cultures through the stories that reflect their unique cultural heritage.

CONTENTS

How Glooskap Conquered the Great Bull-Frog

They began to observe that the brook was beginning to run low. . .
not in the summertime, but in autumn, even after the rains.

1

How Glooskap Conquered the Great Bull-Frog

There lay lazily in the mud a creature who was more of a monster than a man,
though he had a human form.

How Glooskap Conquered the Great Bull-Frog

For he appeared ten feet high, with a hundred red and black feathers in his scalp-lock, his face painted like fresh blood with green rings round his eyes, a large clam-shell hanging from each ear, a spread eagle, very awful to behold, flapping its wings from the back of his neck, so that as he strode into the village all hearts quaked.

3

How Glooskap Conquered the Great Bull-Frog

All the wishes uttered by men are granted. . . . for the first became a Leech,
the second a Spotted Frog, the third a Crab, which is washed up and down
with the tide, and the fourth a Fish.

How the Toad and Porcupine Lost their Noses

So the Turtle went down to the sea; he caught a great whale, he bore it to camp;
it seemed to him easy to do this.

How the Toad and Porcupine Lost their Noses

He put on the shape of an old squaw . . . and sat down by two witches:
one was the Porcupine, the other the Toad.

The Story of Grizzly Bear and Beaver

There was a great lake close to Skeena River, where many beavers built their houses, because it was
deep water and a safe hiding-place and good shelter for them in wintertime.

The Story of Grizzly Bear and Beaver

Now, the great Grizzly Bear's beaver meat was all gone, and the great dreadful thing was very hungry.
He was walking around the lake, searching for something to eat.

The Story of Grizzly Bear and Beaver

"What are you doing there, poor animal?" Thus said the proud Grizzly
Bear when he saw her sitting on the end of an old log.

The Laugh-maker

He climbed a tall pine from whose bushy top he could observe all that took place.

The Laugh-maker

The Laugh-maker was hairless and wrinkled like a new-born child; it had the funniest feet, or hands, or flippers, with which it tried to walk, but only tumbled and flopped about.

The Laugh-maker

He fitted a sharp arrow to the bow and pierced the little Laugh-maker to the heart.

The Daughter of the Sun

Now, the Sun hated the people on the earth, because they could never
look straight at her without screwing up their faces.

The Daughter of the Sun

The Little Men made medicine and changed two men to snakes,
the Spreading-adder and the Copperhead.

The Daughter of the Sun

The young woman was in the outside circle, and as she swung around to where the seven men were standing, one struck her with his rod and she turned her head and saw him.

The Daughter of the Sun

They lifted the lid a little to give her air, but as they did so there was a fluttering sound inside and something
flew past them into the thicket and they heard a redbird cry, *"kwish! kwish! kwish!"* in the bushes.

The Girl Who Married the Star

"Sister," said the Earth, "I have seen a handsome young man in my dreams,
and it seemed to me that he came from up yonder!"

The Girl Who Married the Star

In her haste she struck the ground so hard with the sharp-pointed stick with which she dug turnips, that the floor of the sky was broken and she fell through.

The Girl Who Married the Star

In the morning she found at her side a pretty little boy, a Star Boy, who afterward grew to be a handsome young man and had many adventures.

How Master Lox as a Raccoon Killed the Bear and the Black Cats

Then the Raccoon ran into a hollow tree, the Bear following,
and began to root it up.

How Master Lox as a Raccoon Killed the Bear and the Black Cats

Soon the Raccoon saw the fierce Black Cat, as an Indian, coming after him with a club.

21

How Master Lox as a Raccoon Killed the Bear and the Black Cats

He took it to the river, and, cutting a hole in the ice, put the child into it. The next morning he went to the place, and took out a full-grown man, alive and well. The women were indeed astonished at this.

How Master Lox as a Raccoon Killed the Bear and the Black Cats

Then he came to a great river, and did not know how to get across. He saw on the bank an old *Wiwillmekq',* a strange worm which is like a horned alligator; but he was blind. "Grandfather," said the Raccoon, "carry me over the lake."

How Master Lox as a Raccoon Killed the Bear and the Black Cats

So he went on till he came to some Black Berries, and said,
"Berries, how would you agree with me if I should eat you?"

The Little Boy Man

He-who-was-first-Created at once came forth and took up the infant,
who was the Boy Man, the father of the human race here upon earth.

The Little Boy Man

In those days, there was peace between the animals and the Boy Man.

The Little Boy Man

He-who-was-first-Created now turned himself into a King-fisher, and so approached
unsuspected and talked with the old Beaver-woman.

The Little Boy Man

Then He-who-was-first-Created returned to his own shape,
and with his long spear he stabbed each of the monsters.

The Bear Man

He pulled the arrows out of his side and gave them to the man, saying,
"It is of no use for you to shoot at me, for you can not kill me."

The Bear Man

They went on together until they came to a hole in the side of the mountain, and the bear said,
"This is not where I live, but there is going to be a council here and we will see what they do."

The Bear Man

They fitted the arrow and drew back the string, but when they let go it caught in their long claws
and the arrows dropped to the ground.

The Bear Man

He rubbed his stomach with his forepaws . . . and at once he had
both paws full of chestnuts and gave them to the man.

The Bear Man

Soon they heard the hunters coming up the mountain,
and then the dogs found the cave and began to bark.

The Bear Man

Before they left, the man piled leaves over the spot where they had cut up the bear, and when they had gone a little way he looked behind and saw the bear rise up out of the leaves, shake himself, and go back into the woods.

The Friendly Skeleton

"Well, boy, where do you come from?" The boy told him that he came from the woods.

The Friendly Skeleton

Then the skeleton told him to go to a tree near by, and dig on the west side of it, and he would find a tobacco-pouch full of tobacco, a pipe, and a flint; and the boy found them and brought them to the skeleton.

The Friendly Skeleton

Then the boy jumped into the canoe, saying, "Come, swans, let's go to our place."

The Friendly Skeleton

The boy started and in three days arrived at the rocks, where he found his sister, to whom he called,
"Sister, come, go home with me."

The Friendly Skeleton

He took a stick and commanded her to tell him the truth.

The Friendly Skeleton

The skeleton continued, "Now, gather up all the bones you see and put them in a pile; then push the largest tree you see and say, 'All dead folks arise'; and they will all arise."

LIST OF TRACKS ON CD

1. **How Glooskap Conquered the Great Bull-Frog**
   (Passamaquoddy and Micmac)

2. **How the Toad and Porcupine Lost their Noses**
   (Micmac)

3. **The Story of Grizzly Bear and Beaver**
   (Tsimshian)

4. **The Laugh-maker**
   (Sioux)

5. **The Daughter of the Sun**
   (Cherokee)

6. **The Girl Who Married the Star**
   (Sioux)

7. **How Master Lox as a Raccoon Killed the Bear and the Black Cats**
   (Passamaquoddy)

8. **The Little Boy Man**
   (Sioux)

9. **The Bear Man**
   (Micmac)

10. **The Friendly Skeleton**
    (Iroquois)